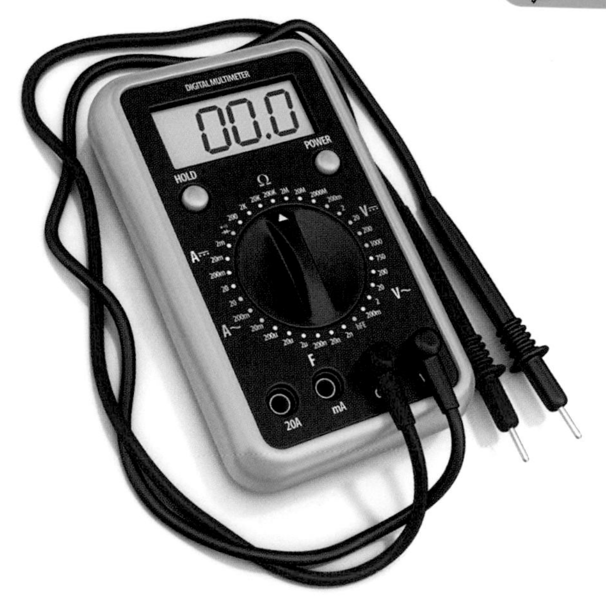

SKILLED TRADE CAREERS

ELECTRICIANS

by Gary Sprott

ROURKE'S
SCHOOL to HOME
CONNECTIONS
BEFORE AND DURING READING ACTIVITIES

Before Reading: *Building Background Knowledge and Vocabulary*
Building background knowledge can help children process new information and build upon what they already know. Before reading a book, it is important to tap into what children already know about the topic. This will help them develop their vocabulary and increase their reading comprehension.

Questions and Activities to Build Background Knowledge:
1. Look at the front cover of the book and read the title. What do you think this book will be about?
2. What do you already know about this topic?
3. Take a book walk and skim the pages. Look at the table of contents, photographs, captions, and bold words. Did these text features give you any information or predictions about what you will read in this book?

Vocabulary: *Vocabulary Is Key to Reading Comprehension*
Use the following directions to prompt a conversation about each word.
- Read the vocabulary words.
- What comes to mind when you see each word?
- What do you think each word means?

Vocabulary Words:
- *apprentice*
- *circuit*
- *install*
- *motion sensors*
- *telecommunications*
- *watt*

During Reading: *Reading for Meaning and Understanding*
To achieve deep comprehension of a book, children are encouraged to use close reading strategies. During reading, it is important to have children stop and make connections. These connections result in deeper analysis and understanding of a book.

Close Reading a Text
During reading, have children stop and talk about the following:
- Any confusing parts
- Any unknown words
- Text to text, text to self, text to world connections
- The main idea in each chapter or heading

Encourage children to use context clues to determine the meaning of any unknown words. These strategies will help children learn to analyze the text more thoroughly as they read.

When you are finished reading this book, turn to the next-to-last page for **After Reading Questions** and an **Activity**.

TABLE OF CONTENTS

ON THE JOB

Do you like figuring out how things connect? Are you good at keeping things in order even when they seem jumbled up? Do you wonder how flipping a switch can make something happen? And do you think power is, well, super?

If you are nodding your head, you probably want to learn more about what electricians do.

A Bright Future!

The United States has about 700,000 electricians—and that number is climbing fast! More homes and buildings are being powered by green energy, such as sunlight or wind. That's powering the need for more electricians.

Electricians understand how solar panels capture the sun's energy to power buildings.

With education and training, electricians can make sense of a maze of wires.

Electricians **install** wires and cables in homes, schools, businesses, and factories. They set up the electrical systems that let us curl up with a good book at night, watch a movie, or pop popcorn in the microwave. Electricians inspect and test equipment, find problems, and make repairs.

install (in-STAWL): to put something into a place where it can be used

What's a **watt**? How do electrical currents flow? An electrician needs to understand how electricity works. That means having good thinking skills and knowledge about science and math. Let's just say you can't keep these professionals in the dark!

watt (waht): a unit for measuring electrical power

Watt Did You Say?

The next time someone changes a light bulb at your house, ask how many watts it has. Then, dazzle with your smarts! Tell them the watt is named after James Watt, a Scottish inventor who improved the steam engine in the 18th century.

LED bulbs use less energy and last much longer than regular light bulbs.

Millions of miles of power lines carry electricity around the U.S.

Electricians work in many industries, including construction, **telecommunications**, and manufacturing. They often work with architects and engineers to design electrical systems for new buildings.

Electricians known as linemen install and maintain overhead or underground power lines. Those lines carry electricity from large power stations to houses and businesses.

telecommunications (tel-uh-kuh-myoo-ni-KAY-shuhnz): the technology of sending messages over long distances by telephone, satellite, radio, or other electronic means

Electricians have been around since before Thomas Edison lit up his first light bulb more than 140 years ago! Back then, the telegraph and the telephone were high-tech! Today, electricians help create smart homes that control power and light with **motion sensors**, voice activation, and the internet.

Thomas Edison

motion sensors (MOH-shuhn SEN-surz): instruments that can detect and measure movement and send the information to a device that controls something

MASTER ON
Tuesday 10:46 am
Home Control
21°C / 69.8°F
920 Kwh
Settings
SECURITY
MEDIA
CAMERA

WHAT'S IN MY TOOLBOX?

Needle-nose pliers grip and clip wires in tight spots. Wire strippers slice away the plastic coating on electrical cables. Glow-in-the-dark rods and fish sticks snag wires that are out of arm's reach! For this skilled trade, you need an assortment of tools at your fingertips. Oh, and don't forget a flashlight —an electrician needs light to work too!

Electricians stay prepared to make emergency repairs around the clock.

Electricity lights up our world. But it also has a dark side—danger! Safety equipment is essential for electricians. They use goggles to protect their eyes and hard hats to protect their heads from falling objects. Insulated gloves and special clothing resist electrical shocks, sparks, and flames.

Code of Conduct

You follow rules at home and at school. Electricians follow rules on the job. The National Electrical Code sets safety standards for all 50 U.S. states. It helps protect people and buildings from harm.

Electricians tap into technology to test systems and discover problems. Thermal cameras find temperature differences behind walls that could be hotspots for trouble. Wireless transmitters send signals to match electrical outlets with the correct **circuit**. Voltage detectors that look like chubby marker pens check to see if power is being supplied to a switch or wire.

circuit (SUR-kit): a complete path made by an electrical current

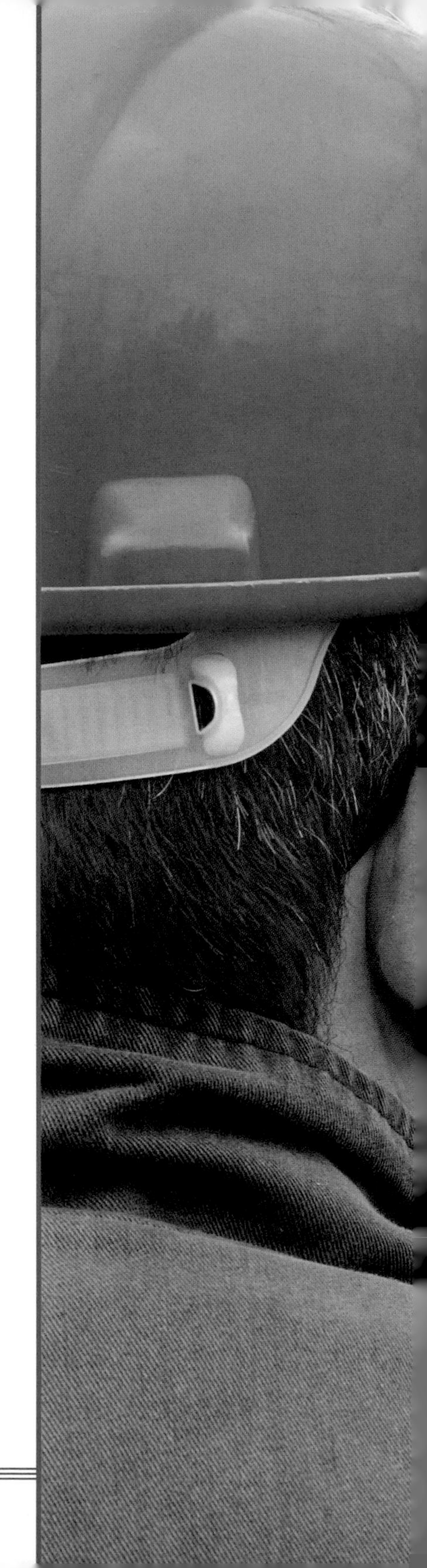

Heat-sensing cameras help electricians spot possible danger from a safe distance.

LEARNING THE TRADE

Has your interest in becoming an electrician been sparked? That's awesome!

There are different paths to this career, and they all start in school. Electricians need at least a high school diploma. Learning subjects such as math, science, social studies, and industrial technology is helpful. So, here's a bright idea: Keep studying!

Apprentices get hands-on experience working with an expert electrician.

An **apprentice** electrician can spend several years learning the trade. Apprenticeship programs include classroom instruction and on-the-job training. Electricians-in-training practice reading blueprints and diagrams, following safety rules, and installing electrical systems.

apprentice (uh-PREN-tis): someone who learns a skill by working with an expert

On the Journey to Master

After an apprenticeship, an electrician is known as a journeyman, or journey worker. But, that isn't the final destination! With extra experience and training, it's possible to reach the level of master electrician.

Electricians often need a license before they can work on their own. They may need to pass a test and have thousands of hours of work experience. Government agencies require electricians to be licensed to keep quality and safety standards high.

All this hard work and training pays off. A master electrician can earn up to 50 dollars each hour.

Solar panels and wind turbines help power cities without harming the planet.

Scientists are searching for planet-friendly ways to make electricity. Green power sources, such as the sun, wind, and ocean waves, produce energy without polluting the air. They help fight global warming and other environmental challenges. Electricians can get special training to become experts in green energy.

For electricians, knowledge truly is power! Electricians must keep learning throughout their career to keep up with changing technology. Luckily, training programs are offered by technical colleges, unions, employers, and other trade groups.

Strength in Numbers!

The International Brotherhood of Electrical Workers has 750,000 members in the U.S. and Canada. The union was founded in 1890, before many American homes even had electricity! Now, it sponsors programs that encourage women to become electricians.

MEMORY GAME

Look at the pictures. What do you remember reading on the pages where each image appeared?

INDEX

AFTER READING QUESTIONS

1. How many electricians are there in the U.S.?
2. Why would an electrician need a glow-in-the-dark rod?
3. What are four types of safety equipment used by electricians?
4. Name three sources of green energy.
5. How do you think the International Brotherhood of Electrical Workers helps electricians?

ACTIVITY

Using less electricity can have big benefits for the planet and our pocketbooks! Think of five ways you can save electricity. It could be something simple, like turning off the lights when you leave a room. Or reading a book instead of watching television. With your parents' permission, do those five things for a month and then check your family's electric bill. Did it make a difference?

ABOUT THE AUTHOR

Gary Sprott is a writer in Tampa, Florida. He has written books about ancient cultures, plants, animals, and automobiles. Gary can change a light bulb. (Okay, most of the time.) And he's really good at telling his wife and daughters to "Turn off the lights!"

www.rourkeeducationalmedia.com

PHOTO CREDITS: page 1: ©pagadesign / iStockphoto.com; page 1: ©xresch / Pixabay; page 3: ©francescomoufotografo / iStockphoto.com; page 4: ©AndreyPopov / iStockphoto.com; page 5: ©LL28 / iStockphoto.com; page 6: ©Andrey_Popov / shutterstock.com; page 8: ©pepifoto / iStockphoto.com; page 9: ©Image Source / iStockphoto.com; page 10: ©nicolesy / iStockphoto.com; page 12: ©Mvuijlst / Wikimedia; page 13: ©andresr / iStockphoto.com; page 14: ©Davizro / iStockphoto.com; page 15: ©JPWALLET / iStockphoto.com; page 16: ©sturti / iStockphoto.com; page 18: ©Shinyfamily / iStockphoto.com; page 21: ©monkeybusinessimages / iStockphoto.com; page 22: ©BartCo / iStockphoto.com; page 25: ©AndreyPopov / iStockphoto.com; page 26: ©narvikk / iStockphoto.com; page 29: ©kali9 / iStockphoto.com

Edited by: Madison Capitano
Cover design by: Rhea Magaro-Wallace
Interior design by: Book Buddy Media

Library of Congress PCN Data

Electricians / Gary Sprott
(Skilled Trade Careers)
ISBN 978-1-73163-832-8 (hard cover)
ISBN 978-1-73163-909-7- (soft cover)
ISBN 978-1-73163-986-8 (e-Book)
ISBN 978-1-73164-063-5 (e-Pub)
Library of Congress Control Number: 2020930172

Rourke Educational Media
Printed in the United States of America
01-1942011937